GOD'S
REPOSITION
TO
POSITION

God's Reposition To Position
Copyright © 2024 by Essie Crockom Roberts

Published in the United States of America

Library of Congress Control Number: 2024916530
ISBN   Paperback: 979-8-89091-673-0
ISBN   eBook: 979-8-89091-674-7

All rights reserved. No part of this publication may be reproduced, stored in a retrieval system or transmitted in any way by any means, electronic, mechanical, photocopy, recording or otherwise without the prior permission of the author except as provided by USA copyright law.

The opinions expressed by the author are not necessarily those of ReadersMagnet, LLC.

ReadersMagnet, LLC
10620 Treena Street, Suite 230 | San Diego, California, 92131 USA
1.619. 354. 2643 | www.readersmagnet.com

Book design copyright © 2024 by ReadersMagnet, LLC. All rights reserved.

Cover design by Tifanny Curaza
Interior design by Don De Guzman

GOD'S REPOSITION TO POSITION

Essie Crockom Roberts
Revised Edition

I dedicate this book in loving memory of my father, Mr. James Crockom, a deacon of the church for many years, and my mother, Mrs. Lillie V. Crockom, a strong, longtime prayer warrior. They both turned in their swords for a perfectly fitted crown in 1978 and 1990, respectively, but not before they made sure that their six children were introduced to Jesus Christ as Lord and Savior at early ages. They lived a godly life by setting an example before their children and giving instructions in the Word of God to live a holy life unto God. I still miss and love them with my whole heart. Thank You, Father, for my wonderful, loving, and caring parents.

ACKNOWLEDGEMENT

MY SPECIAL APPRECIATION TO Mary Nobles and Phil Heckers for their faithfulness to believe in the vision God placed upon my heart, in addition to their steadfastness in prayer, encouragement, and loyalty to God and the ministry.

I give special thanks to my three birth brothers, Thomas, John, and Pastor Robert Crockom, who have nourished, protected, and loved me unconditionally, supported me in the ministry placed on me by the Lord, and have been father figures to me since the homegoing of our parents.

I am stronger and better in this life because of these extraordinary men.

INTRODUCTION

THIS BOOK WAS WRITTEN under the leading and guidance of the Holy Spirit. The intent is to inspire the reader not to stop mid-course on your way to purpose or give up on the call of God for your life. Maybe you feel stuck, tossed, unsure or even on hold, concerning God's plan for your life. It perhaps could be that God is repositioning you to a greater position for the fathering of His character in you. Stopping in the midst of transition may cause a malfunction.

Every past experience you had was once a present choice. Seeking God will always cause you to make right choices in life, but even if you make the wrong decision, continuing to seek God will lead you to the paths He's carved especially for you. Better and better is just a few steps away; you must remain focused. Giving up on God should never be an option for the believer. Instead, stay strong in the Lord. Sometimes we think we have arrived, and we get too comfortable. Then God has to reposition us yet again into position (His will).

Habakkuk 2:2–3

"And the LORD answered me, and said,

'Write the vision, and make it plain upon tables,

that he may run that readeth it.

For the vision is yet for an appointed time,

but at the end it shall speak, and not lie:

though it tarry, wait for it;

because it will surely come, it will not tarry.'"

Chapter 1

HEARING WITHOUT EARS

He that hath ears to hear, let him hear.
(Matthew 11:15)

THE GOSPEL RECORDS IN Matthew 11:15 and 13:9, Mark 4:9, 23, and many other places in the scripture: *"He that has an ear to hear let him hear" (let him pay attention and understand)*. What do you do when you've heard God speak, knew exactly what He said, but fail to realize His word would come in stages? The fullness would come in pieces, not all at the same time, and because you heard and were excited to hear, you started the journey in obedience, not considering what the end would be. It is continued obedience that will get you to a perfect ending.

God uses the usable. Being used by God is a tremendous honor. Absolutely no one can make use of your availabilities in search of profound order as can the Creator. God takes the time to fine-tune us. If we sway away from His frequency, we are no longer spot-on connected. Position yourself to recognize the uniqueness of God's call and special assignment in your life.

Carrying out His task, we may face criticizing comments, rejection, or even threats, especially when we obey the call. Others may not understand or agree with us. Just know that it is obedience to God that really matters. Make it a top priority to obey Him. Who can travel the road given to you by God, except you?

The road can sometimes be long and lonely. Rest assured you are not alone. He's your constant companion on every rocky road. God on the high mountaintop will continue to be God in your lowest valley. The valleys are great opportunities to spend time with the Father; that will enhance your spiritual growth. They offer a good time to pray, seek His face, and allow your heart to be still before Him. He is always ready to lead and guide your inside mind away from any captive mode or method created by the enemy. God can and will reshape your every thought.

To hear naturally, there must be an opening of the ear carnal gate. The physical ear is that part of the body which serves as an instrument which allows sound to travel through, be it music, words, alarm bells, animal noises, rushing waters, or airplanes in the sky. The human ear is positioned on the side of the face, for the purpose of hearing sounds.

He who has an ear, let him hear (pay attention to and understand) what the Spirit is saying. For the believer, the natural hearing ear, positioned on the side of the face, has nothing to do with and cannot be compared to the hearing that comes by way of the Holy Spirit's supernatural ability to transform us. This ear has the ability to hear what the natural ear will never be able to comprehend. Stay tuned; don't touch that dial. Stay on this frequency; there's more to come. You are being fine-tuned.

Consider this: even trained animals know how to focus on their master's every move, with eyes and ears trained on their master's presence. Even with eyes closed, they can sense and respond with an incredible ability to hear. In the same way, we must discern the presence of the Holy Spirit, tuned into Him at all times, fine-tuning our hearts to sense and respond to His leading.

He will speak in ways not attuned to normal hearing. Tune out sounds that are taking up your hearing space, anything that hinders your spiritual hearing -- the clear sound wave coming from the Father. He will pull you out of the external, carnally minded slave labor camp. For all things written to take place, you must now hear His voice. Begin to resist the tendency to replay in your mind any recordings of limitations that your family, friends, background, or environment may have created for you in your past.

The enemy began working early in my life to place every hindrance he could conjure up to block my spiritual hearing. Growing up, I accepted Jesus Christ as my savior at age eleven, living at home with my mom and dad. There were many rules in my father's house, one being that if you lived under his roof, you must serve his God, that being the Lord and Savior Jesus Christ. My dad was a strong father figure in our home. His children did what he told them, whether they liked it or not.

During that time I had no idea there was a call on my life; such a thing never crossed my mind, and why would it? I didn't know what a call was except maybe a summons to dinner, or by friends to come out to play. I was the youngest of six, well protected by the elder ones. Things began happening to me for which I had no explanation, for instance:

- In my early teens I had a condition called rheumatic fever, which landed me in the hospital for some time. Many weeks, I missed most of one semester of my seventh grade year in school. Praise God, my grades were at a 4.0 average, high enough that I was not held back, still able to make the next grade.
- Between the ages of thirteen and eighteen, I was subjected to three rape attempts, on three separate occasions by three different pastors.

- The enemy tried to take my life in two unrelated car accidents.
- My mother and father, as well as a brother and two sisters, went home to be with the Lord. I still miss them today.
- I was abandoned by my husband after twelve years of marriage; later, he also went home to be with the Lord.
- Every material thing I'd ever worked for as an electrical designer was lost, even my home, cars, jewelry, self-esteem, and much more.
- I was homeless for two years.

The enemy cannot hold you in any trial of his. God will not allow His children to experience anything for which He has not prepared them to endure to the end, and that endurance will bring its own rewards.

There hath no temptation taken you but such as is common to man: but God is faithful, who will not suffer you to be tempted above that ye are able; but will with the temptation also make a way to escape, that ye may be able to bear it. (1 Corinthians 10:13)

For I reckon that the sufferings of this present time are not worthy to be compared with the glory which shall be revealed in us. (Romans 8:18)

Chapter 2

HAVING HEARD

LIFE'S REESTABLISHMENT BEGAN AFTER life's brokenness. For two years, day and night, I sat by the fire of the Word of God, renewing my mind and gaining godly knowledge. My life was totally altered both spiritually and physically, and it took on new meaning.

Then I was picked up from one state and moved to another before I knew what was taking place. Suddenly I was in new surroundings with new people, renewed in spirit and with a fresh outlook. Unbeknownst to me, God had beforehand put everything in my life in His divine order. I became connected with a new church and new people.

Among the people I came in contact with after some time at this church were some strong, faithful prayer warriors and intercessors with tremendous callings to fulfill. We formed a bond and began gathering on occasions for prayer. For a considerable amount of time, we would pray for many concerns of life, the body of Christ, the nations, families, and friends. These faithful ones were ready for whatever the Holy Spirit was leading us to do.

In 2005, God instructed me to establish a ministry. This word came not from any person to me, but directly from the Spirit of God. It then became apparent why God had given me such a sizable home through this transition. When the Father pulled me off my job, never did I dream that it was for full-time ministry. I thought it was because He knew I was tired of the heavy workload of the corporate world and a tedious travel schedule and wanted to give me some rest. Of course, the Bible does say that He knows the plans He has for us. It's possible if I had known what He had in mind for me at that time, I would have chosen to stay on that tedious job. Thank God, I did not know, and only He knew the plans He had for me. Nevertheless, the ministry was established in the basement of my home.

During that time, a ministry friend of mine flew in from California for a weekend of rest and relaxation. She was instructed to take lodging at my home. From the time I picked her up from the airport, we began sharing our present seasons of what we believed God was doing in our lives. I shared with her what the Spirit of the Lord had revealed to me, concerning taking the ministry forward and that I was tarrying for more clarity.

Later that evening, she suggested that we go down into the basement to pray. We began to pray the prayer of agreement, and what a great explosive move of the Spirit of God followed. His plans for the ministry began to unfold. For the entire weekend we were listening and getting instructions on how to proceed, as we tarried in the presence of the Lord.

After some time, I later approached the other prayer warriors with what the Spirit had placed in my heart; more agreement was set in place. We were off to a wonderful start, and the ministry was established and began to grow in spirit and in number. Some close friends introduced me to an apostle from England who was overseer of a number of churches there. We shared a meal together in my home, and for approximately eight hours we were all together in the basement, praying and receiving imparted gifts and messages.

For three years, the basement of my home was home church. Many came together to fellowship weekly. It was a glorious gathering of the saints. Excitement was in the air, and growth was on the move. At the end of the third year a burning desire of the Holy Spirit on the inside began to impress upon the ministry it was time to take the next step, to begin believing God for a building with more room.

The search began. We looked at a few prospects over a period of months, but none was what we wanted or could afford for the number of members we had. The membership was enough to fill the basement of my home, but a building was out of our natural comfort zone, something new and different for us. Faith in God means trusting in His ability and not our own. We had heard from heaven, and that was all we needed, so we started the journey of looking for a building.

One day, while driving back home from an appointment, I caught sight of a certain building that was for lease in the very same area and street in which I believed I'd heard and felt the leading of the Holy Spirit. I continued to drive past the building toward home. The Holy Spirit instructed me to turn the car around, go back, and inquire about the property. Sitting in front of the building, I put in a call to the telephone number listed on the sign. No one was available to take my call, so I left a very brief and simple message. That was it; I had done what I was instructed to do. To my surprise, the very next day, my call was returned, and an appointment was set to view the property. Within three days, negotiations had given us the opportunity for a three-year lease option. As we continued to pray concerning the matter, things were falling in place in our favor. I heard the Holy Spirit say, "Take it, it's yours," even though the expense was far beyond what we expected or could afford.

Please keep in mind we were coming from a basement in my home with a membership large enough to fill the basement, but a building was a different matter. Faith sometimes means reaching higher than your own limitations or the boundaries you set for yourself, to just believing in the abundant, limitless abilities of God. He can and will bless in ways unimaginable.

We signed the contract and moved in with a minimum of red tape. We had put funds aside for expected financial obligations, and were we ever excited! The spirit was high, and the anointing was incredible. The members were growing in spirit and the knowledge of God.

Strangely enough, after seven or eight months, we discovered the membership was not growing in numbers. We were trying everything we knew to build the church's attendance, but it was not happening. At the end of the first year, the church's income took a turn for the worse. I began using my personal savings for the upkeep of the ministry. Later, others began giving from their personal funds in addition to their tithes, time, and talents in an effort to help keep us afloat. When my savings ran out, I then took out a loan on my car, acquired two personal loans, sold most of my jewelry and anything else I could get my hands on, in an attempt to meet the obligations of the lease, while trying to maintain the spiritual vision of the ministry. It is a tremendous load on a leader if one has the task of building the church spiritually as well as serious concerns about accelerating debt and bills against reduced income.

The building was located in a commercial mall with common parking. After gaining the knowledge that we were a church, the other tenants wanted nothing to do with us, nothing to do with God or with God's house. The enemy began to set up its rage against the work of God. Raging spirits of witchcraft, jealousy, control, and hindrance emerged, as well as unbelievable attacks of confrontations over parking rights. One time, a plucked dead bird was placed at the front door of the church. Just to name a few other strange things, the outside lighting worked irregularly, and the air conditioning system was unstable. Nasty-looking watchdogs were set up against the surrounding parking lots. The rooms were always freezing cold, never mind how the thermostat was set.

The one thing that was working was the hand of God. We knew we were working with a word from God. When you know you've heard from heaven, you continue to stand through it all. Especially when there is a strong resistance in the assignment, standing becomes a part of the assignment.

One very cold, snowy night in December, the temperature dropped to far below freezing. A water line broke in one of the rooms on the north side of the building. The water flow ran all night, flooding a very large portion of the building. A great portion of the walls, ceiling, floors, furniture, and equipment were damaged, so much that the building was unusable for seven weeks due to damage and repairs. My thinking was taken up with what was happening at the time—the building being flooded, the lagging finances, and of course the rage of the opposing spirits—at the same time as I tried to keep focused on staying with the original word given to us by God. I was not aware a shift was taking place. I now believe it was during that period God began speaking of a new thing, a fresh work.

However, I was holding on to what I knew I had heard Him say to me one year before. In the year past, my hearing was fine-tuned to what He was saying then, but somehow I had not remained tuned in to know what He was saying presently. It seemed as if God had made a shift when I was asleep and did not inform me. Suddenly I was awake, and He had moved on. God turned a corner, whereas I had remained on a street that was a dead end.

I heard this on TV ministry: "A bend in the road is not the end of the road unless you don't make the turn." I missed a turn. My focus was on the word given me at first when I saw the for-lease sign. At that time, He said, "Take it, it's yours," but later the full knowledge of the complete revelation escaped me. I did not realize that it was a for-that-time word and that things were subject to change as deeper knowledge would be revealed.

Seasons change, time moves on, but God is always and forever. I now know that the flood and the finances shortage was an indication to move on: "It's over, this phase is done." Something new was being formed.

It brought to mind the remarkable move of God in the life of the Prophet Elijah.

> *And the word of the LORD came unto him, saying: Get thee hence, and turn thee eastward, and hide thyself by the brook Cherith, that is before Jordan. And it shall be, that thou shalt drink of the brook; and I have commanded the ravens to feed thee there. So he went and did according unto the word of the LORD: for he went and dwelt by the brook Cherith, that is before Jordan. And the ravens brought him bread and flesh in the morning, and bread and flesh in the evening; and he drank of the brook. And it came to pass after a while, that the brook dried up, because there had been no rain in the land.*
>
> *And the word of the LORD came unto him, saying: Arise, get thee to Zarephath, which belongeth to Zidon, and dwell there: behold,*

I have commanded a widow woman there to sustain thee. (1 Kings 17:2–9)

When God told him to get to the brook and camp, *there*, God did not mention that the brook would run out of water supply at any given time. God was saying to Elijah that the brook named Cherith was the place for him to be at that very time, because provision was there. Elijah was there for some time enjoying the cool fresh brook water and the daily delivery of meat and bread by the ravens. I'm sure he had no idea the brook would soon be drying up. Then provision was gone from that place. The place called *there* had moved, but provision relocated itself to the new place called *there*. God did have a plan for Elijah's continual supply and provision. He never said, "Elijah, I've changed my mind." He simply said, "Elijah get up go someplace else." Provision made a shift. Did God change His mind? No, He just gave further instructions.

Elijah was moving by faith as God led him. It was obvious Elijah had heard clearly the new directions. He began to follow point by point. He heard and did just as he was instructed. His hearing stayed tuned to the voice and leading of the One doing the providing.

I believe that God's provision is confirmation you are operating in your assignment. It's not a test because you've been bad; it's to see what you have learned from the teacher. Everything you go through will become an opportunity for spiritual development.

Finally, seven weeks later, the building was repaired from the flood damage, and we were back in the building, very excited to be back. Everything was fresh and new, and we were happy. You see, for seven weeks, we relocated back to my home and truly missed the building and all its comforts, but being back in the basement did not help the attendance. Members drifted away during those seven weeks. Great efforts were made to contact everyone with the good news, that it was time to return to our building. Some seemed no longer interested in supporting the ministry, but that didn't stop us from moving back into our beautifully renewed place of worship.

Over the next two months, the church's financial situation seemed to be faring well. The Holy Spirit was strongly present, and the members who remained were excited. The facility was improved and, in fact, better than when we first moved in.

By the beginning of the second quarter, finances began to sink again. Membership giving was tremendously low, and attendance was down. We really never had a large membership, but always with the help of God were able to meet our financial obligations. But we had reached the point where, regardless of how many invitations we sent out to visitors and to the community, none showed up. Banners were placed on street corners on Sunday morning announcing service date and time, balloons were in front of the building to catch the attention those driving by, and we even had a spot on a local radio station. It seemed every financial door was shut tight. We tried getting a loan, to absolutely no avail. We had not been established long enough, nor did we have the adequate membership to qualify for the loan.

At this point, we were down to five faithful members and had become desperate. We were behind on our monthly lease payment, and things were tense, stress was high, and money was down. We knew the Father was hearing our prayers and saw the condition we were in; we just could not figure out why He was not answering.

We were sure we were doing what God had led us to do. At the forefront of our minds was that God's wisdom was doing the best thing at the time, in the best way, for His best purpose in the life of the believer. However, in our quest to please the Father with obedience, we never noticed that the place called *there* had dried up. We were no longer in sync with what or where the Lord was leading and not recognizing we were no longer in step with the Holy Spirit.

Soon the enemy moved into the camp. It's become difficult to follow the leading of the Holy Spirit when He's moved on and you are still in a holding place, waiting to hear from Him. When you're out of place, there is no covering. We were all alone, on our own. The landlord became very controlling and offensive. The church was located in a strip mall, and the tenants next door wanted nothing to do with God. There were sexual sins, witchcraft and everything else you could possibly imagine going on behind closed doors. They wanted nothing to do with the Spirit of God.

Those evil spirits did not stop there. Some of them affected the congregation by way of a leader in the church who had struggled with the spirit of control and pornography in the past but had for years been delivered and truly rededicated to Christ. Somehow the enemy had begun pulling on his cause within the struggling vessel, and the old wounds were reopened. The controlling spirit from the landlord, along with the sexual sins and witchcraft from the tenant next door, had resurfaced and showed up in the leadership of the church, thus spreading in secret, hidden corners.

My physical and spiritual being was under a draining attack. A resisting force from the inside joined forces with the resisting forces on the outside, workings its hindrances of envy, witchcraft, and jealousy. We were unaware that the warfare we were fighting on the outside of the congregation was now on the inside. The three forces of sin then joined forces in a fight against the ministry, which was to say there was no fight at all. With God, we win. He was in control and had been all along. The Father had made every decision concerning us for our good.

We needed a new "now" word. God's word had worked for Joshua in marching around Jericho's walls, and knowing that He is the same yesterday, today, and forever, we were sure that if God's word worked for Joshua, then that same word would work for us.

The Holy Spirit instructed us to release the building, which was once a blessing and had become a very heavy burden. We marched around the building as if we were in Joshua's army. We did it six times, and on the seventh time we shouted and released the building back to the Lord, praising God for what He had done. The very same day, immediately after we had completed marching followed by an intense praise service, the landlord placed a three-day pay-or- quit notice on the front door of church. Yes indeed, the place called *there* had truly made a shift; a transition had taken place.

Have you ever felt like your "brook" has dried up and God is nowhere to be found? God caused it to dry up. There were signs all along the way, saying this well is dry. We missed the signs by not allowing the old things to come to an end and pass away, by not being open to the new ventures ahead. It was His doing all the time.

He had us to go there just as He had spoken to Elijah to go there. The mistake we made was in our own minds, assuming He would never tell us to go someplace, only to have us leave that place for someplace else that was not in our plan, in order to further provide.

Understand this, Elijah never talked about the brook when he arrived at the widow's house, never said, "The reason I'm here is that the brook ran out of water." He knew he was there because provision had relocated to another place, the widow's house. He knew obedience was his only hope of unlocking the supernatural provision of God. The purpose at the widow's house was for Elijah's continued provision and for deliverance of the widow's household. Whatever you go through in life is designed to aid others in their life's effort. Her meal barrel and oil multiplied, and her son was revived back to life. It was not only about Elijah; it was about the needs of others. God was not just blessing Elijah. He was now using him to be a blessing to others. When the widow obeyed God and released her meager supply, all she had, God intervened in her circumstances and released His supernatural supply for her household. Elijah had an ear to hear the Spirit of the Lord whenever He spoke to him. I believe he was hearing from God in ways most were not accustomed to. He did precisely only what he heard and was directed to do at that time.

God's Reposition to Position

If you are married or have a close spiritual connected relationship with someone, think of the ways you communicate with each other without speaking with your voice. It's an eye contact, a facial expression, a gesture of the body, or maybe a style of walking. Whatever it may be, the other gets the message through your expression. They can understand what you are saying without words coming from your mouth. When our relationship with God is in its proper position, with the aid of the Holy Spirit, we can then hear all that the Father articulates. He who has an ear, let him hear.

The three-day pay-or-quit notice was posted on the door; it was time to go. There was no money in reserve or otherwise. There was absolutely no other financial resource to draw from in that place at that time. It was a bittersweet moment for us.

The Holy Spirit led us into a releasing mode of prayer. In order to be able to move forward into the new, we had to release the old. Sitting in my office at the church, a staff member and I began praying to God for His guidance, inquiring what would be the next step.

After we let it go in the spiritual realm, there was still the natural to deal with. The building was filled with office equipment, furniture, appliances, nursery and kitchen supplies, electronics, a huge warehouse, and accessories. It was the weekend; our manpower was down to only two available members to help with moving things out of the building, and no storage arrangements had been made. We had three days to get the building cleared out, Friday being one of those days, and it was late Friday afternoon.

We were operating in fast mode faith. God gave wisdom enough for us to know that we truly needed His help. So we sat not in panic mode but in prayerful mode, continuing to pray to the Father, not moving until He gave directions. The Holy Spirit began to instruct. We pulled out the yellow pages of the phone book and began calling storage places and used furniture stores to see if they would be interested in purchasing or taking items on consignment. Knowing the deadline of the departure date, we continued to apply our faith in God. Never, ever underestimate the power of God. The Holy Spirit will give clear directions when you acknowledge Him in all your ways. There will be no confusion; He's not the author of it.

There was an advertisement in the yellow pages which said "we buy furniture." I proceeded to call the business. The man who answered identified himself as the owner and said that his business normally did buy furniture but was at an overstock high at the time and did not have space to receive any more furniture. However, he gave me the name and number of a business associate who might be able to assist me.

This turned out to be the blessing needed at the time. I immediately contacted the person. As we talked, he asked a few questions and then said, "I'll be there right away." The time of day was not advantageous for driving, as it was rush hour, and his office was located far on the other end of town.

God sent help in as if He had organized a special army to battle just for us. The power of God began to operate like an unstoppable herd of cattle. The gentleman walked through the door with his hearing opened to the Holy Spirit of God. He introduced himself, referring to himself as Reverend, and from that point forward, we were out of control and the Holy Spirit was in control. The reverend stopped talking in the middle of our conversation, sat down, and began speaking in a heavenly language with his body bent over to the floor. Then he asked if we could pray together.

He stated that the Holy Spirit was speaking to him in a way he'd never heard before. He did not know anything about us, yet the Spirit was at that time instructing him to accommodate us in whatever we needed. I explained the urgency of the situation to him. He then offered us free storage for all the church's furnishings and the manpower to make it all happen as soon as possible. Of course, we accepted.

The next day, manpower and moving truck was at the door. In two and a half days, the building was cleared and cleaned. What a God-sent and prayer-answering moment! The next day, it really felt like a huge burden had been lifted. We never paid a penny in storage fees. There was still the issue of some other outstanding debt. Within several months, God had supernaturally wiped the debt slate clean.

He who has an ear, let him hear. Wouldn't you know, the landlords came back and asked us to please consider moving back in after they had kicked us out, admitting they had made a mistake. We said no; we were free. Later on, we got information that the landlords were unable to acquire another tenant and were losing money on the building; eventually, they lost the place.

God the Father instructed me to bless the reverend and two pastors whom I'd never met, nor did they know each other. I was to bless one with the belongings in storage (furniture, appliances, etc.), and the other with the electronic equipment, by giving and sowing into their ministry. These two pastors were deeply moved by the blessing from God. They were both pastors in beginning stages of building their new ministries, and at once, they were given all they needed to begin their congregational meetings. Even more, the reverend with the storage business allowed both congregations to hold their church meetings in a part of his facility. Three ministries were supplied and provided for by what one ministry began with.

Being confident of this very thing, that He which hath begun a good work in you will perform it until the day of Jesus Christ . . . (Philippians 1:6)

What had begun was not lost; it was continuing through three new ministry sources. God's message for us had become very clear: direction and provision had moved, but we were to stay tuned. He who has an ear to hear, let him hear. God speaks to those who are prepared to listen, who make Him their top priority. Don't let the radio be on but you're not hearing, or the song playing and you're not listening.

Chapter 3

WHO SAYS YOU HAVE TO STOP?

AN OVERNIGHT STORM CAN seem to last forever when walking with God, but when the rain stops, the wind ceases, and the flood is over, God will have washed all the debris from your life and given you a clean and clear vision of what it is He wants to remove before the promised blessing shows up in your life. If the blessing shows up before the storm is over, it could be washed away in the storm. The blessing might never be recognized as a true blessing. The storm was the setup for the blessing.

Disappointment will arrive; heartaches will visit; trouble will try to linger around your door. So what? Who says you have to stop moving forward? Every journey has its lows and highs, but faith is able to override time and natural circumstances.

God is absolutely dependable, in every circumstance, in any situation. Trust Him; with one blink of His eye, your situation, no matter how hopeless it may seem, can change. God sets the stage, and all the props are in place, so that you may live the life He has purposed for you.

Your worst enemy is sometimes working right beside you, seeming to be in agreement with you but actually working against you. The enemy is not so visible all the time; he can come dressed with the right apparel, speaking the right words, doing the good works, scriptures in mouth, bible in hand, joining in prayer sessions and bible study, and never missing a meeting. He does not forget the giving of finances to make it all seem legit.

He has an agenda. He's been in a back room planning a strategy, developing a plan to accomplish his satanic assignment against you. Sometimes he comes as a small tender plant, growing and increasing slowly, gaining your confidence to trust he's really there for your good. Whatever you do, don't run little errands that are connected with his way of living. Don't give him a vote in the way you conduct your life.

Sin has no dominion over the believer. We are not under any manmade law; we are under true grace through the shed blood of Jesus Christ, our Lord and Savior. It is the kindness by which God bestowed His favor and blessing upon the ill-deserving, you and me. It's free, no charge. The fool has said in his heart, there is no God. He thinks he will never be exposed.

Apply your faith. Where doubt, uncertainty, and unbelief flourish, faith is absent. Faith in God gives you complete access to His power—faith in God, not in human strength. Every spirit that's not of the Holy Spirit must submit to the spirit and power of God within you. When you get to know Him well enough and want to know Him badly enough, He'll show up.

Your understanding will solidly be under God's authority. You will advance because you've been commissioned by the Holy Spirit. He will perfect that which concerns you. You are the winner, called, chosen, and appointed. God wants to express Himself in and through you. He allows all the old wood to burn off the bad edges from your life, so who said you had to stop?

> *He delivered me from my strong enemy, and from them which hated me: for they were too strong for me. They prevented me in the day of my calamity: but the LORD was my stay. (Psalm 18:17–18)*

> *Trust in the LORD with all thine heart; and lean not unto thine own understanding. In all thy ways acknowledge Him, and He shall direct thy paths. (Proverbs 3:5–6)*

Praise Song to God

How Can I Ever Leave You, Lord?

You've held my hand
You've pushed me
You've carried me
You've led me
You've fed me

You've been keeping me.
I now know, You've been constant
How can I ever leave You, Lord?
When others asked, how did I make it?
My answer, I was carried by the Cross Bearer.

No one ever held me like You
No one ever pushed me like You
No one ever carried me like You
No one ever led me like You
No one ever fed me like You

Your love is breathtaking.
How can I ever leave You, Lord?

A Love Song to God

Romance Me, Lord

Show me things I've never seen before
Take me higher than I thought
I could ever go
Tender mercies, Lord, I see
Reigning in me by Thee.
Romance me, Lord Hold me, Lord
Bear me up in Your love.

Essie Crockom Roberts

The Grace Song

Without the Hand of God

*The hand of God was there holding
back the hammer of time,
To teach me a lesson that could only be mine.*

*The clock was ticking, no hope in sight.
I sat waiting, pondering in mind,
Ready to take over and leave God behind.*

*With mercy on one side saying,
"I'm giving you time to repent" and
Grace on the other telling me
"I'm your defense."*

*Then in came Jesus and removed the hammer
of doubt and despair.
For without the hand of God,
I would have been there.*

*So I thank You, Lord, for Your hand that wouldn't
Let me be me, for Your shield
between me and the enemy.
When my foot slipped, Thy mercy held me up.
For You protected my mind and
called me into Your time.*

Here are some scriptures that can help you on your path from reposition to position. Meditate on these for a little while.

Ephesians 1:17–20

That the God of our Lord Jesus Christ, the Father of glory, may give to you the spirit of wisdom and revelation in the knowledge of Him: the eyes of your understanding being enlightened; that ye may know what is the hope of His calling, and what the riches of the glory of His inheritance in the saints, and what is the exceeding greatness of His power to us-ward who believe, according to the working of His mighty power, which He wrought in Christ when He raised Him from the dead, and set Him at His own right hand in the heavenly places.

1 Corinthians 2:9–10

But as it is written, Eye hath not seen, nor ear heard, neither have entered into the heart of man, the things which God hath prepared for them that love Him. But God hath revealed them unto us by His Spirit: for the Spirit searcheth all things, yea, the deep things of God.

Proverbs 2:10–11

When wisdom entereth into thine heart, and knowledge is pleasant unto thy soul; discretion shall preserve thee, understanding shall keep thee.

Psalm 27:1

The LORD is my light and my salvation; whom shall I fear? The LORD is the strength of my life; of whom shall I be afraid?

1 Corinthians 1:3–5

Grace be unto you, and peace, from God our Father, and from the Lord Jesus Christ. I thank my God always on your behalf, for the grace of God which is given you by Jesus Christ; that in everything ye are enriched by Him, in all utterance, and in all knowledge;

1 Peter 1:3–4

Blessed be the God and Father of our Lord Jesus Christ, which according to His abundant mercy hath begotten us again unto a lively hope by the resurrection of Jesus Christ from the dead, to an inheritance incorruptible, and undefiled, and that fadeth not away, reserved in heaven for you,

Hebrews 12:1–2

Wherefore seeing we also are compassed about with so great a cloud of witnesses, let us lay aside every weight, and the sin which doth so easily beset us, and let us run with patience the race that is set before us, looking unto Jesus the author and finisher of our faith; who for the joy that was set before Him endured the cross, despising the shame, and is set down at the right hand of the throne of God.

Philippians 3:14

I press toward the mark for the prize of the high calling of God in Christ Jesus.

ABOUT THE AUTHOR

ESSIE CROCKOM ROBERTS WAS born in Shreveport, Louisiana, and accepted Jesus as her Lord and Savior at the early age of eleven. She moved to Pasadena, California, in her teen years, where she attended Pasadena City College and Cypress College. Later, she attended School of Design Methods, Hollywood, California, for engineering and electrical design. Her career background is in electrical engineering, which she practiced for over twenty-eight years.

Her ministry is that of a call to testify of the gospel of grace of God wherever she goes, whose faith does not stand in human wisdom but in the power of God. Though she was never blessed with biological children, God turned it for good, blessing her with an abundant array of spiritually blessed children.

She studied, promoted, and participated in street evangelism for many years.

She is the founder of A Place of Worship Ministries in Littleton, Colorado.

Essie currently resides in Littleton, Colorado. This is her first published book.

ABOUT THE BOOK

THIS BOOK WAS WRITTEN under the leadership and guidance of the Holy Spirit. The intent is to inspire the reader not to stop halfway on his path to purpose as well as to not give up on the call of God for his life. Reading this book will encourage you to keep an open ear to the voice of the Spirit of the Lord. It's designed to lead you into all truths. Be willing to go all the way with the Lord.

CONTACT THE AUTHOR

By email

essrob@comcast.net

Healing sometimes come immediately or it can come, by the way of a process, connected to a journey ordered by GOD.

- Essie Crockom Roberts

MORE RESOURCES FROM THE AUTHOR

YONDER WONDERS: LIFE CHANGING REVELATIONS

Reading Yonder Wonders will help you polish your life with the newness and freshness of the Holy Spirit within you.

This book was written under the leadership and guidance of the Holy Spirit. It will inspire the reader not to stop on his or her way to purpose or to give up on the call of God. This book will encourage the believer to keep an open ear to the voice of the Spirit of the Lord because it will lead to all truths.

Believe in bigger and better things. Gather new visions, create new goals, and dream greater dreams. The dream on the inside wants to connected to the outside to become a reality and manifest itself.

Every experience you've had in life was once a present choice. Seeking God will always cause you to make right choices in life. But even if you make wrong decisions, continuing to seek God will lead you to the paths that carved distinctly for you. You're just a few steps away so remain focused. Never give up on your belief in God. Stay strong in the Lord.

MORE RESOURCES FROM THE AUTHOR

FEAR IS NOT FOR YOU: STEP AWAY FROM TORMENT

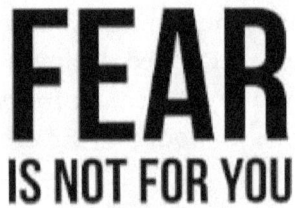

Fear tries to override and establish itself in the earth that God, Himself made. Heaven and Earth was spoken into existence by and with the love of our Heavenly Father. This book can help you eradicate, do away with, exterminate, erase, get rid and completely uproot all forms of fear, that could possibly have you in bondage, causing you not to live life to its utmost development. God is LOVE, not fear. Allow the love of God to point you to a tormented free life.

www.ingramcontent.com/pod-product-compliance
Lightning Source LLC
LaVergne TN
LVHW041554070526
838199LV00046B/1961